RLS

AT THE WORLD'S END

RLS

AT THE WORLD'S END

STEPHEN SCOBIE

Ekstasis Editions

Published in 2009 by:
Ekstasis Editions Canada Ltd.
Box 8474, Main Postal Outlet
Victoria, B.C. V8W 3S1

Ekstasis Editions
Box 571
Banff, Alberta T1L 1E3

LIBRARY AND ARCHIVES CANADA CATALOGUING IN PUBLICATION

Scobie, Stephen, 1943-
      RLS : at the world's end / Stephen Scobie.

Poems.
ISBN 978-1-897430-32-3

      1. Stevenson, Robert Louis, 1850-1894--Poetry. I. Title.

PS8587.C6R58 2008   C811'.54   C2008-907671-0

RLS: At the World's End has been published with the assistance of grants from the Canada Council for the Arts, the Book Publishing Industry Development Program (BPIDP) and the British Columbia Arts Council administered by the Cultural Services Branch of British Columbia.

Printed and bound in Canada.

*I saw rain falling and the rainbow drawn
On Lammermuir. Hearkening I heard again
In my precipitous city beaten bells
Winnow the keen sea wind. And here afar,
Intent on my own race and place, I wrote.*

RLS,
Weir of Hermiston

*Loved of his land, and making all his boast
The birthright of the blood from which he came,
Heir to those lights that guard the Scottish coast,
And caring only for a filial fame;
Proud, if a poet, he was Scotsman most,
And bore a Scottish name.*

Richard Le Gallienne,
Robert Louis Stevenson: An Elegy

"Out of my country and myself I go," sings the old poet.

RLS,
The Amateur Emigrant

RLS

AT THE WORLD'S END

I am the son of the evening. Listen,
here in Samoa, on the farthest west

side of the world, my rising hour is the last
of the global day. By the time

this reluctant morning of mine
has raised its weary head, tomorrow

will be advanced along
its grey Presbyterian hours

into Edinburgh's evening.
And I'll be behind

by a dozen pages:
Tusitala

whatever tale I'm writing
or poem I am not yet finishing

over the cusp of the newly
time-zoned world.

Robert

Lewis

Balfour

Stevenson

— you'll be saying
it's a fine name, a rich

succession of syllables,   But I
moved into it slowly, uncertainly,

adopting each one
at a slow, considered time:

Robert, never Bob (or God
forbid me, never Bobby);

Lewis, later Louis
like a foreign king (I never

pronounced it that way, but I chose
the spelling);

Balfour, for my kidnapped
Whig inheritor:

and Steven's son. There in that name
my whole life lies defined.

Owned and disowned. Oh,
like the Jack of Diamonds, please

play my card, and
forget my name.

The winds are still
quiet this evening:

waiting for the storm.
Tonight this whole Pacific island

huddles down, and the groaning branches
ache already, in a slow

anticipation. Long before morning
the proudest will be scattered, torn,

random on the forest floor,
strewn with tributes.

     Oh but I know
     those high pale towers

     on that farther
     side of the world

     will stand the storm.

     There on Skerryvore
     and the bare Bell Rock

     they will assert
     their presence, and my father's name

        Stevenson
        Steven's son

     against this rising wind, against
     this long and human gale.

Let there be light
said my father, like

all fathers before him
to the start of time:

let there be light
and there was

        light
        house
        keeping

on those desolate
scraps of land

reefs and ridges no one
had dreamed to build on

until my father, and
my father's father

white stone towers
erections of dreams

against the wild
and battering sea, old ocean

surrounding salt, and the long
beseeching of wind.

You in my dreams forever

father of darkness
father of light

old ocean.

Imagine a room
in a dour house
on a Scottish street:

dark room
dark house
dark street.

There must be a dresser in this room,
solid, with many drawers,
secret and hidden, furniture:

and a writing desk,
where fathers and sons through
generations planned

the family
projects, all
those stately Stevensons

carved to the finely fitting of
intent and inclining bodies,
dark

designing hands.

Under the red sky
Smout lies discarded,
greetin' like Columba's horse, until

Cummy comes, to hold me tight,
inside her grasp
of hellfire and reluctant

heaven; stories screaming
through all my childhood years
of sleepless nights, my

coughing hours and dim
Presbyterian dreams:
Edinburgh evenings

a sickly child's
garden of verses
versus

weeds, thistles, stinging nettles
rank undergrowth of dock and fern
everywhere bad children go

who do not have
the luxury of
great fathers, rich fathers

those who build, who bring their light
to the scatter of storms
angry on our ragged edge

of a marginal country: kidnapped
Scotland.

I don't want to
go to Hell

I don't want to
go to Hell

it's very simple
Cummy tells me

I don't want to
go to Hell

be a good boy
like a Christian

be a good boy
Cummy tells me

be a good boy
go to Hell

Cummy tells me
very simple

like a Christian
I don't want to

say my prayers
Cummy tells me

night is falling
I don't want to

very simple
go to Hell

[…]

say my prayers
I don't want to

Cummy tells me
night is falling

say my prayers
go to Hell

Louis, not Lewis; changing
the name but not

the pronunciation: just try
reading that line aloud.

Scottish or French, or
Jekyll and Hyde:

listen to all the voices
calling me down the years:

Lewis
Lewis
Louis

father, mother, dearest nurse
I hear you even from the farthest

south Pacific. Listen: Lewis
is coming home.

One thing, indeed, is not to be learned in Scotland,
and that is the way to be happy.

        RLS,
        The Amateur Emigrant

You can't really, Louisly,
enjoy yourself in Edinburgh.

Drink is only another darkness
you steep yourself into

one dark staired wynd
after another,

or else the New Town's
draughty parallelograms.

Of all the cheerful clubs
I was the orator

good for any topic, but excuse me
not for a song, no

I never was one
for the singing of old

Jacobite dirges
sodden with heather.

Burns excuse me,
I was never

a lyrical lamenter
of ages past and gone.

[…]

My medium was prose
and I pursued its measure

all these nights of solemn drinking
in the grey cold tenements

at the world's end.

My Father who art not in Heaven

Continued be thy name

May your lighthouses shine
according to your blueprints
on the storm-swept reef as on the shifting sand

Give me my measly monthly allowance

And pay all my debts
as I incur new ones

Be horrified by my temptations
and pray intently for my straying soul

For Heriot Row belongs to you

The family firm, and the family name

At least for now.
                    Amen.

I'd say that in Scotland the weather
is never small talk:

"a fine forenoon" is a grave
considered amelioration;

"miserable times we're having"
implies we deserve them

and must passively tolerate
meteorological judgement.

"A fine day, is it not?" includes
the possibility of "not."

But when the sun
grants a hesitant embrace,

then the old stones of Reekie
soak in its warmth, and haud it dern

even in cellars, and in winding stairs,
letting it go

in grudging January, or
capricious April, till

a boy and a girl
huddle in Princes Street Gardens

telling each other small talk, "warm
for the time of year," and cuddle closer

into the promise of the cold
and lucid, northern light.

I came to my early stories
slant, no heroes, no great men

performing epic deeds,
but rather

small, decent, homebody folk
caught up and tempted by

a sense of adventure, a small
itch of dissatisfaction, a snag

of loose thread in the even weave
of their hodden grey

sensible lives.
And suddenly in their hands

a pirate sword, a Rajah's diamond
and the world is full

of colours, bright and threatening,
the kind you see in dreams, but now

streaming down Princes Street,
coming right at you.

What are we Scots? We're scarcely
a single nation, living in yoke

Highland and Lowland
Saxon and Gael

under Her Gracious Majesty, that sad
and lonely woman who would rather be

a German Countess. Our history
divides us rather than unites us:

it was none other than ourselves
in our best dress uniforms

who hunted our Prince through the heather
into his alcoholic grave, God rest

his haunted songs and his stubborn soul.
But the one

trait we can always find to share
is our long and absolute

disdain of England. Foreign nation,
pallid tongue. — I know that people say

I am, of my age, the greatest
English stylist. But I would say

I am a stylist (whatever that may mean)
in English, not *of* it.

I write it always as a foreign tongue,
hiding in its elegant precision

while the unregenerate Scot in me
stumbles through that bloody heather

pechan and sweitan, disjaskit, forfeuchan and broun'd-aff.

May the guid Lord gang wi ye
an keep ye peace

May his troubled Grace let fall
slow countenance upon ye

the dern face o the dowie Lord
shine blessings on ye

and on yir cairt, and on yir dug
and on yir wee bit clartie cat

that sleeps awa her leelang hours
afore yir silent

television

I might as well be shoving a donkey's arse
up some French mountain road

as trying to tell you this: dear Reader
I care about you.

I care how well you're feeling, I care
whether you had a decent breakfast.

I care about what you're wearing, does that
waistcoat really suit you?

Is there a bright and sufficient light
that sheds on my page? Are your rubbing your eyes

out of weariness, or bleared displeasure? Are you sitting
down in your easy chair?

The road to the top of this mountain
is long and dusty, smeared by sun.

The donkey, by its nature, is recalcitrant.
It's a long hard climb

to the bottom of this page.

Give me one breath of the last
idiot wind

blowing through the north
far north

country of my cold
imagination: let it catch me

climbing over rooftops, sliding
down slopes of perilous

grey slate, onto the East Coast
crow-stepped gables, all

to capture some evasive clue
to that hidden treasure

island —

of which, once I sail away, I will leave
no trace, no map

for any man to die for, neither
Doctor nor Squire, nor

Pew, Blind Pew — not even
lost in the daze of rum

my captain, Billy Bones.

Lays the Black Spot
on Billy Bones

image of his deadlight eye:
Blind Pew

comes stumbling up the stony path
(the way up and the way down

are one and the same)
into the story

following the map
I idly drew. And I too followed

to the secret place of burial
which of course proved empty.

No one there
to receive the stigmata:

Bones and Pew and all Flint's crew
scattered to memories.

Only the Sea Cook left, the seafaring
man with one leg, Barbecue,

and someone tells me
he's gone to Sweden: well,

if the old bones roll,
God rest his soul.

The start of the story, in the house
called Admiral Benbow. This lined old seaman

Bones W. — he might as well
have been an Admiral

as what he was, God rest his soul, a pirate.
The one who survived

even Flint. May the good
Lord forgive him. Though drink

and the Devil did for him
soon enough, and no one has seen fit

to tell his story. Was that really his name,
Bones? Billy Bones?

He may stand on the shore with a spyglass to his eye
scanning the horizon

but that doesn't help him survive my story
beyond Chapter Three.

Treasure Island: or
How I Learned to Kill

and be proud of it.
You take a boy of

undetermined years,
set pistols in his hands

— hands, hands,
Israel Hands — does it help

to call him a Jew? —
just watch me

trapped in the rigging
knife through my shoulder

and the whole ship
reeling beneath me

Hispaniola

squeeze these triggers,
see him fall —

Lewis, how many fell
into that clear

and crystal water?
Louis, how many fell?

The last outback
at the world's end — it wasn't really

that filthy pub on the so-called
Royal Mile. It was a corner

of my wretched soul, one
and infinitely divisible:

Jekyll and Hyde.

Later, all the good people would say
my life was drunk away

in Edinburgh howffs.
It was never that simple.

When I think of this soul of mine,
I see double, double as always.

There I am standing, a fop
with a silk tie saddled

high around my neck, like a noose.
And beside me is the man with one leg

standing on his stump, and holding out
— for balance, or for pardon —

two warm and
bloody hands.

Israel hands.

Oh, *Treasure Island*, it was all
for my father. It was every story he told me

on winter evenings in Heriot Row, when he stood
in the narrow doorway of my bedroom:

with me, but not coming in.
Now I told the story back to him

in that cramped cottage in Braemar
on sodden Deeside — while down the road

our gracious black-clad Queen was sulking
over her own long death and dying — and my father

came to each evening reading of my daily chapter
as eager as a schoolboy for his lesson

or for his father's love.

I was born on one black morning
as early as the rain
I saw the sun come rising
familiar as my pain

The city slept inside its dreams
which could not be untold
No Scotsman uttered any word
whom already had been sold

I saw the sun in Reekie's lift
as yellow as a curse
I watched the nation's loyalty
decline from bad to worse

I never called Surrender
I always cried Attack
I sailed for Treasure Island
and never could come back

But the treasure never followed me
It stayed where it is bound
The X marks but an empty spot
where nothing has been found

The treasure's always Scotland
It hides in Reekie's lands
It echoes underneath your feet
It slips between your hands

I was born on one black morning
My father coughed and swore
Another light of Scotland was
erected on his shore

Great God of All My Fathers! —
please forgive me

for what I'm about to say:
you are Most Merciful, and yet you are

sometimes in my mind
but a wee bit scrap

of cloth cast off
into a woman's basket

which some day she may sew
into a plaidie's pattern

or else it may lie, abandoned,
until the Gathering Day

— You

treasure of all my world.

Fanny invaded me, her visions
conquered my mind.

I felt as if I had become
suddenly unfinished, like a sketch

of a French wood, Barbizon,
the pale bark of a leaning poplar,

just a few quick dabs with a wet-laden brush,
outlines on paper. But green

the essence of green;
and I felt my own existence hang

for the breath of an eye
in Marvell's "green shade" —

no longer Lewis, but a cautious
sketch of Louis, provisional, defined

by this strange
American woman

dressed all in black, advancing
invading the frame

shoving the trees
into the background —

so I found myself
like a schoolboy carving

> *for Fanny*
> *RLS*

onto a tree that existed
only in my mind, like a sketch

of Barbizon.

I see you, see you, see you
on the banks of the Seine.

To me, you are all this city:
I must rename every street

to bear your signature,
and every bridge on this grey

forgiving river. Even the wind
which whispers "I love you"

to each and every
stone on this island,

even the wind
has learned your name

and repeats it to me under
my broken breath.

Yet all the time I am making
love to you, I am visibly

dying. It goes on so long
we become accustomed

to the morning
coughing up of blood,

to the evening
coughing up of blood.

I lie here, nothing more
than a complication of coughs and bones.

I have composed my own casebook;
I am my most experienced physician.

Let me talk myself out
of this world, as surely as

some good Scots doctor talked me
into it.

Writing in bed. I became a reluctant
expert. Hours a day, and

all my years. The trick is
to catch the angles:

first of my own
cough-racked body

propped against pillows, which
cramp the lungs, and press the pain

down

into the back. And then,
the angle of the writing board

leaning along my knees, with the hand
sloped against paper

and following the timeless track
into the margin. Last,

of the bottle of ink, dipped into,
which must preserve its balance,

guard against spill —
lest it obliterate

the white of paper,
the white of sheets

rendering both page and bed
uniform black, illegible.

Not quite steerage: "second cabin"
— just enough distinction

for a brass plate on the bulkhead to remind me
I was a gentleman. Even when Ireland

vanished with a hoarse low cough
into the clouds astern. And then

there was only time and the sea. Even time
was growing changeable. We had to persuade

one good Scots lady that her Glasgow watch
would not tell New York time. All she could say

indignant and disbelieving, was
"Gravy!"
                    — to which our kindly laughter said Amen.

***

One miserable stowaway was found
in a dying state among the fuel,

uttered but a word or two, and departed
for a farther country than America.

***

And then the emigrant train
crept like a snail across

the plains of Nebraska
the desert of Wyoming

[…]

closer to the woman that I loved
farther from all that I called home

a line of moving misery
across the chasm of myself

my own familiar desert, west
into the sunset of my soul.

What I loved in San Francisco
was the fog: fog that could give

even the East Coast haar of Edinburgh
lessons in sheer

tangible damp. The Golden Gate
stayed firmly closed. Night airs

whispered from Alcatraz, and soaked
into whatever remained of

my lingering lungs. Dry desert wind
was close enough — New Mexico,

legends of the Rio Grande — but I
was stuck on the California shore

no doubt because
I wanted to punish

my homesick lungs with memories
of a true

deep Scottish damp.

Fanny, it's I'll come looking for you
all the way
to California

Fanny, it's I'll be sounding after you
all the way
to the abandoned gold mine of my heart

Fanny, it's I'll be climbing after you
all the way
up stairs and narrow wynds of Reekie

Fanny, it's I'll be rhyming after you
all the way
through a shuffled ream of legal paper

and the paper is my heart
and my heart is the city
and the city is my far imagined shore

Once, living in Monterey, I was firing
target practice with a Colt revolver:

fine figure of the Old Wild West.
One bullet jammed in the barrel

and like a fool, I fired again
and again. And again.

Six bullets in all, each one
witness to a stubborn Scots stupidity

till the barrel was choked
from muzzle to breach

with smoking lead. Just one more shot,
the gunsmith said, and I'd have lost

my life, or at least my hand —
my writing hand, that is

which would come to the same thing.

Was it always sideways
she used to watch me

never the one
to be too sure?

Slept in silence
when the night wind whistled?

Laid down her book
and waited in the dark?

If I gave her another name
Catriona

was she any closer than a guess
a tune I misremembered

singing in the night?

And then, my dear, we got married:

standing stiffly
side by side

as if it all meant nothing:

your disappearing husband
your re-appearing children

and in my proper Edinburgh
Thomas and Margaret

praying for toleration.
Ah, but you and I

you and I, my dear

we are the winds on the mountain,
we are the silence on the plain.

Davos: the clean sharp air
cuts into my lungs
with a surgeon's knife. The sun

burns into the snow, until its white
dazzles your sight, scorches your eyes
like cloth scrubbed on stone.

Along the valley, perched on the slope
like patient pigeons, goatherds' huts
preserve the words of shelter,

deep-smelling hay. They scatter
as if flung by a casual hand
across the incline. And the air

chills, sings a high song on
the summits of scale, descant
of notes that echo into

what Davos has to tell David
of mountains
and high liberty.

Hyde and Jekyll, Jekyll and Hyde:
that goddamn book

is going to haunt me
to death and beyond.

I wish I'd never written it. No one
can talk of anything else. And they all

assume I am who I write about, that I have
within me a hidden Hyde

(how could I have chosen
such an obvious name?). No I won't

go to see the stage version,
nor the movies to come. I want rid of it,

I want it buried back
in the Edinburgh depth

from which it came.

Och man, I'm a sick man
in Bournemouth, o aa places

for the love o the leal!
I'm a man wha cannae breathe

in France, in Switzerland,
on the taps o fashionable mountains

far less in an English town
by the wicked sea.

Aa the bienly air is my enemy:
whit I breathe best is reid Scots bluid.

I'm no a man for ony age, I ken that noo:
my measure has been taken

closer than a gloaming's thocht,
tighter than a deerskin drum.

Oh My Lord
my sweet lord

it's when I'll be thinking
when I'll be looking

up into that evening
red sky watching

how small am I
or rather, how large am I

in all your creation?

larger than a lighthouse
smaller than the man who built it

Lord forgive me if I ask
such a question

or, if You designed me to ask
such a question

who designed You?

It's not yet late, the night —
and the stars scarce spent.

I can still from my darkened window see
Orion hang his hunter's sword

low from that triple belt,
and Cassiopeia spread

her wide and stellar W
up from the dark horizon.

Hours are left to me yet:
Fanny has gone to bed, I sit alone

and the bland Bournemouth night
hums and ticks and breathes and whispers

into the lyric of my lungs.
The paper underneath my pen

is damp with sweat, and my forehead also
drips as I bend

words to the desperate page:
David in the heather

sleeping (far more readily than I)
under his hunter's sky, which still

has worlds to swing
hours to measure

afore we can say

> *home is the sailor*
> *home from sea*
>
> *and the hunter*
> *home from the hill*

It's an unco long road that goes
up that mountain in Samoa

to the place I will build
myself for refuge,

but maybe you'll be thinking
in your inner heart

it's not much longer than other
roads I've taken:

remember my boy David, and the hard
Highland roads I sent him on

by day's end staggering
another weary lang Scots mile

into a doubtful shelter. No,
it's the truth I'll tell you —

all roads are long, and the way steep,
and the footing treacherous: heather

and tripwires in the heather, David
brother of mine.

The sun beats on this hillside
of far Samoa, each and every

leaf breathes perspiration into
the morning's gathering heat.

Yet my old
cough comes clattering, as if

[…]

you and I, Alan, were still at a crouch
on a hillside in Appin, with the great

grey green of bracken hiding us
from the road, from the long road

down.

How did you get your actors to fall
so drastic and convincingly? the film

director was asked. Easy, he replied:
tripwires in the heather.

That's the way I did it too: I cheated.
Gave them all kinds of

verbal tripwires: "a King's name,"
puckered Whiggery,

every predictable pitfall Scotland's
history presents. Alan too proud

for any other way, and David
decaying into decency

as fond as a barnyard pig
under the hired hand's snoodling.

God help him, he set his sword
against his right and legal

Hanoverian succession. He took
for officer his foreign King's

absolute name, and stuck
like a Scot on a point of honour

dying, as like as maybe,
on the Bass Rock, jinking

the steady history of birdshit
coating his scabbard.

King George! and leave aside
all the names of all the glens:

finally undo
three hundred years

into the long east coast's
white wavering,

fallen to silent scratching out
of sounds we were never

meant to hear: the diamond
screech of the owl

in the dark
wood's echoing. The fox:

Alan Breck.
Alan Breck Stewart.

May your name live forever
in the green of the bracken,

in the depth of the glens.

It's true now, true as I e'er can say
that the Campbell is deid

— ye hae my word, as true's a Whig,
and Alan too —

aye, Alan Breck, however much
he wished the deed, it wisnae his

hand on the trigger. He may well have
"a grand memory for forgetting," but let me

bear witness for him: I am the word
that cannot be spoken, or

I unspeak aathin'
that's gaen afore me

and I'm standing
in the line of fire

not so much a witness as a target
an inconvenient truth

with nothing to protect me but
my stubborn honesty, my

guid Scots name.

        I am, my Lord, your most
        obedient servant,

        David Balfour.

God rest me from those who would tell me
how to breathe: as if my lungs

had no kent wisdom of their own, no experience:
as if I could not consume

Davos like a steak of venison
gulping it down

body/blow/body

breath of my new
gasped rhythm, telling me

the damaged measure of my lungs
which yet could take me

out beyond Gourock
Firth of Clyde

only the high
Atlantic waiting.

Henry James sent a case of champagne,
delivered to the ship. That's grand —

we'll drink it all on the voyage out,
toasting the high Atlantic, launching

each empty bottle to the lonely waves: a dozen
mute yet heartfelt testimonials

to the master's regard, to his measured prose,
to the ocean which divides and joins us.

One bottle each evening, drunk to the King
"over the water," and to Henry James:

God bless his paragraphs, his semi-colons;
God bless the distinguished air

of his long Atlantic love.

After the ocean, New York was madness.
A city in which everyone had read, or at least heard of

"Jekyll and Hyde," and wanted to meet the author,
shake his hand, and take his money.

I tried escaping to Central Park,
the end of the Mall (a bonny spot) and there

I found myself suddenly
hemmed in, surrounded, overseen:

two statues, brooding together,
the ghosts and overlords

of my imagination.

       Sir Walter Scott and Robert Burns.

As if all the load of my inheritance
had followed to mock me here.

Sir Walter at least is close to earth, looking down
with an intense frown,

burdened by the debts of Abbotsford.
A doting dog looks up at him.

Burns is the sentimental ploughman, gazing
heavenward for inspiration, a quill pen poised

as if he never read a book, or
worked at a draft

but waited for some Muse to strike
between two rows of barley.

[…]

How long have I struggled with these two, or wished
we could drink together, all night in Edinburgh

at the World's End. Instead
they track me down in New York City

and I am caught
between their implacable bronze.

I'm going back to my hotel
and the Jekyll journalists.

The journalists tell me
I must myself be torn

between Jekyll and Hyde — aye,
and not a few

of my friends think the same. If only
it were just that simple.

In the first place, I'd say
there was Scotland, the double country

with its dozen different
Presbyterian Jekylls

and even more Hydes
than you could bite your thumb at.

On which side are you counting
my esteemed parents? Or Cummy

with her nightly tales
of hell and damnation?

More than ever, here in America
it's the tongue I speak

that tells the maist, this somewhile Scots
that gangs far deeper

than when I write
my fine and proper

English prose.

[…]

In Scots I just bauchle along
doun a weel-kent road

an gin the bogle Hyde
rises afore me

I bid him guid day
a brither by-passer

someone I recognise
someone I know.

Preparations for a Pacific voyage:

the Captain took one look at me and ordered
gear for a burial at sea;

asked what he would do if my mother
(sixty years old in her starched black mourning)

were swept overboard, he answered:
"Put it in the log."

Let the sky be a single colour:
what I'm used to

is Edinburgh Presbyterian grey,
but I'll settle

for a strident Pacific blue. What I can't
thole, are these multi-

variegated shades of
Samoan twilight: when the sky's deep bowl

of blue, dimming, fashes itself
into hints of green, then sinks

to purple, tones of red, and smooths itself
across the tender globe, while sometimes it seems

pure white
flashes across the firmament. Too much

for me to deal with. I know
where I am with grey. I'm walking along

Edinburgh High Street, where stones and sky
hold between them a grave

conversation of equals. Grey,
says the sodden sky; and, Grey

concurs the considering stone.

Auld Reekie — black as the soot
that's grained into your stones —

*black as a footprint
in shining hallways,* the old

song has it: and the lands of Reekie rise
forever and always, to the sun

soiled, a dirty smudge across the sky,
shuffling sideways like a country loon

into another day, another law-suit,
the city by your leave petitioning

its own existence, *before the Easter
as I was kneeling.* Remember

the wildness of those evenings
I walked your failing streets, Auld Reekie,

city set on a hill
for all to see

your high and Calvinist divinity
which darkens, not illuminates

those narrow wynds, those dowie lands —
darkness is your only door —

and the High Street climbing up, back arched
like a cat about to pounce

on one of its own
abundant rats.

[…]

You are my city still
here in Samoa, when on a clear

pure morning's breeze, I still cough up
the blackest bile: it is your air

I am breathing; the soot that stains
my linen, is your leaving:

city of sinking dreams,
dearest and darkest

it was you that blackened it
forever and always.

I never needed a map
of Edinburgh, no

nor street signs either.
The High Street was simply

the High Street, and I knew
each wynd and close and stair

by its name and by its shadows, not
by any words on paper.

I made my errant way
one turn at a time; at any corner

the slant of my shoulders
would be my guide

and sure enough, there was an open door
and a woman smiling.

Ach man, it's fine I ken
that naethin happens in *Catriona* —

just a daft Whig lad
caught on the points of punctiliousness

unable to speak his straight Scots mind, far less
act out his desire. A prisoner

on the Bass Rock, no just for a couple of chapters —
the whole bluidy book! I must have been reading

too much Henry James, to write a whole novel
without any action. Now, you may say

I wrote it for money, and I'll
no say I didn't. Poor David's story

had nowhere to go but backwards —
back into Scotland. Firth of Forth. And to write

here on this humid hillside, a thousand things
growing around me that I cannot name,

to write about Scotland: man,
it was purest pleasure

like a clootie dumpling

like a streak of heather

like a lamplighter's evening cry
on an Edinburgh street.

May the night's warm night
bend over me

like the comfort of a long
forgotten song: the words that come

and come again, over and over,
the chorus, what we call in Scots

the owrecam.   Words repeated
until the heart

knows them by heart, and the song
sends you to sleep

in a moment's whisper. God,
I wish it was so easy!

I who, ever since a child
(do you hear me, Cummy?)

have lain awake
at 2 and 3 and 4 a.m.

waiting for the hint of light
that will calm my breath

and let me sleep.

> *And aye the owrecam o his lilt*
> *Was, wae's me for Prince Charlie*

Well I'll be damned
here comes your ghost again —

Mister Hyde, only this time
the *Reverend Doctor* Hyde

smearing the pieties of our sect
over a dead man's corpse and name.

"He was not a pure man
in his relations with women" — God damn

Damien!

And over the rampart cliffs of Malakai
the living dead, the lepers, lift their song.

Life is looser in the islands: time
stretches itself like a fireside cat

and men grow lazy, let things slide.
The old grim forms of law (which I once studied)

improvise and fudge distinctions.
A man can contract to a marriage

for the span of one night, and send his bride
to hell in the morning. And I've heard tell

of a wedding sworn, not on the Bible
but on a copy of *Jekyll and Hyde*

— which I of course deplored. Largely because
it was a pirated edition.

The Master of Ballantrae

dying and being reborn
born again and then re-dying

over and over, as if death

was but a nursery toy
that Cummie gave me

and which I
with all my generosity

could never bring
myself to give back —

not in the dark
of a Scottish midnight

nor in the mystic garden
of this strange New World.

Down along the cove
Samoan music:
Pacific waves, the gentle

insistence of rhythm,
a warm night gathering
hesitant breath

but more and more
it is Scotland
inscribing its memory

its dying destiny
grey encircling
the weight of inheritance

down along the cove
where the planet's waves
whisper their name

in the secret tongue
of the lost river, of the final glen,
of the heretic loch.

I'm shivering with heat
here in Samoa's

tropical colours, letting the world
the ordinary yellow world

go by. For a while
I've decided not

to see yellow: banished
are daffodils, the memory of daffodils

and the strident song
of a hillside of gorse. No more

of that primary clamour
into the prism's eye:

and wallpaper, take this
yellow wallpaper

out of my room! Then tell the cook
(but be very tactful

when speaking to the cook) be careful
how you use saffron.

I can taste yellow.
It's not a colour Scotland intended

for the tongue, for the palate, for the
gut. Don't even talk to me

about bananas. In my dreams
there is a ship approaching

[…]

which tries to fly the flag
of welcome, but can only show

the yellow flag of fever: passengers
who would extend a hand of friendship

shake and tremble. Refuse them, let them slip
forever between islands

into the chartless
Yellow Sea.

I don't have to call some
Viennese doctor to tell me

sons and fathers
fathers and sons

all over my work
dead or missing, absent fathers

finally, here in Hermiston, the father
judicially killing his son

Father, I have killed you
again and again

Father, I have taken your place
and made it empty

Where you built light
I have shone darkness

I cough and cough
your name into that darkness

old ocean

my soiled inheritance
you are the end of light

Fanny, it's I'll come sounding after you
all the way
to far Samoa's twist of time

as I have followed you
and you have followed me
these twenty years —

we never settled down
in placid Edinburgh's
douce grey streets

but lived on shattered hillsides
tumbling oceans
exiled islands —

now we are at the rest
of all our wanderings:
travellers' home.

Fanny, it's I'll come sounding after you
all the way
to far Samoa, and beyond.

Vailima, where I built my final home:
the long verandah measuring

my pacing feet. High on the mountain,
looking to the sea. Had I but world enough

and time, I could sail to Scotland.

Vailima, where the chiefs built me a road:

the Road of Loving Hearts
the Road of Gratitude

because I helped Mata'afa, they helped me
hacking and clearing and digging their way

up from the shore.

Vailima, place of the Five Springs:
where a young girl carried water (*vai*)

cupped in her fingers (*lima*) to her chief
where he lay on the mountainside dying:

just like Tusitala
Writer of Tales.

Tonight as I sit in Samoa
with all my family, my friends,

my servants — I cannot make
these fine distinctions — tonight I know

this is forever. Oh, I've played the games,
pretending I'll can still go "home," but Scotland

has slipped away from me like a morning mist,
like a song's "night visitor,"

and left me in its place
Samoa, island of all

first and final possibilities, where now I know
I will live and will die: on this hot hillside

with its humid air
squeezing the breath to my reluctant lungs,

some afternoon
no doubt I will be writing, and the page

remain unfilled: I see myself
not falling, but standing up

with a strange and terrible
rushing of blood to my head

and if it please God, one moment
of grave lucidity

in which, yes, I will indeed gang hame
and the tall grey lands of Reekie

precipitous city

will stoop and kneel and bow
and bid me welcome.

*It seemed unprovoked, a wilful
convulsion of brute nature…..*

NOTES

These poems inhabit, obliquely, the voice of Robert Louis Stevenson (1850-1894) — or rather, they form a dialogue between that imagined voice and my own. (As an internal dialogue within one voice, they are perhaps not unlike *The Strange Case of Dr Jekyll and Mr Hyde*.) The poems are, however, deeply fictional, and, while they draw upon many elements of Stevenson's life, they make no claim to historical accuracy. I have taken many liberties with the chronology (*Treasure Island* comes rather too early); and I know that these poems follow only a narrow path through the wide landscape (and seascape) of Stevenson's life and work.

Among the many, very many books on Stevenson, the one that I have found most useful is Jenni Calder, *Robert Louis Stevenson: A Life Study* (Oxford University Press, 1980). Also quite essential is *Selected Letters of Robert Louis Stevenson*, ed Ernest Mehew, (Yale University Press), 1997, an incredible and inspiring volume.

My title has three possible references. Samoa is indeed "at the world's end." It stands on the edge of the International Date Line. When Stevenson lived there, he was quite literally at the end of the world, where one day had ended and the next had not begun. (Samoa adopted the International Date Line in 1892, two years before Stevenson's death.) RLS himself uses the phrase in his letters.

Secondly, there is in fact a public house in Edinburgh, on the High Street, called The World's End.

Thirdly, Bob Dylan's album *Modern Times* concludes with the line "At the last outback, at the world's end," itself an unacknowledged quote from Ovid. There are many unacknowledged quotations from Dylan in these poems: let this one acknowledgment stand for all, and may Dylan lovers have lots of fun spotting all the other ones.

page 7   "Tusitala" was the Samoan name adopted by RLS. It is usu-
ally translated as "Teller of Tales," but, despite the alliteration, it
is more accurately rendered as "Writer of Tales."

9   The "Pacific Island" is of course Samoa. But it is also Vancouver
Island, where I live. This poem was written on an evening when a
heavy storm was predicted.

Skerryvore and the Bass Rock were two of the isolated islands of
stone on which RLS's father and grandfather somehow contrived
to build lighthouses. My own great-great-great-grandfather
worked with the Stevenson firm. "Skerryvore" was also the name
RLS gave to his house in Bournemouth.

10   "light/house/keeping": a nod here to Jeannette Winterson, and, at
a farther remove, to Marilynne Robinson.

"old ocean": Lautréamont, via Godard (*Weekend*).

12   "Smout": pet name given to RLS as a child.

"Columba's horse": legend has it that St Columba's horse, meet-
ing its master on what was to be the day of the saint's death, burst
into copious tears of premonitory mourning.

"Cummy": pet name for Alison Cunningham, RLS's nurse, to
whom *A Child's Garden of Verses* is dedicated.

16   "draughty parallelograms": RLS, *Edinburgh*.

18   The conflict on religious views between RLS and his father came
to a head with a furious quarrel in 1873.

21   "pechan and sweitan, disjaskit, forfeuchan and broun'd aff":
"panting and sweating, worn out, exhausted, and fed up." From
"Sisyphus," by the great mid-20th century Edinburgh poet Robert
Garioch.

25 First four lines repeated from an earlier poem of mine, "Black Circle" (1980).

"Stonypath" was the Dunsyre home of Ian Hamilton Finlay, who frequently invoked the quotation from Heraclitus.

"he's gone to Sweden": Björn Larsson, *Long John Silver: The True and Eventful History of My Life of Liberty and Adventure as a Gentleman of Fortune and Enemy to Mankind* (1995; translated from the Swedish by Tom Geddes, 1999).

27 "undetermined years": nowhere in the text of *Treasure Island* does RLS specify Jim Hawkins' age.

In *Treasure Island,* the one man killed by Jim Hawkins is named Israel Hands.

"just watch me": Pierre Elliott Trudeau, 1970.

30 "whom": the grammatical incorrectness here is borrowed from Bob Dylan.

32 "Barbizon": mid-19th century school of French landscape painting, named after the village of Barbizon, near the Forest of Fontainebleau. RLS's cousin Bob spent summers at an artists' colony in Barbizon, and it was in the nearby village of Grez-sur-Loing that RLS, in the summer of 1876, met his future wife, Fanny Osbourne.

34 "a complication of coughs and bones": RLS, *Letters.*

36 This poem is based on incidents recorded in *The Amateur Emigrant* — indeed, the second section is a "found poem," quoted directly from RLS's words.

39 "sounding": while this word carries its normal meanings of making a noise or measuring a depth, I mainly use it in the sense of moving urgently towards something, as in the Scots ballad "The

Bonny Earl of Murray":

> Oh lang may his Lady
>   Look frae the Castle Doune
> E'er she see the Earl o' Murray
>   Come soundin' through the toun.

40 This incident is reported by RLS himself, in a letter to W.E. Henley, 1879.

43 "Davos": sanatorium in the Swiss Alps. It is generally assumed that RLS suffered from tuberculosis, and these poems, in their descriptions of his "damaged lungs," adhere to that image. However, Roger Robertson writes:

> "the length of his survival … and the lack of any transmission to those who lived in such close contact with him make [TB] seem unlikely. More probably it was hereditary haemorrhagic rupturing of the blood vessels (HHT) (as Alan Guttmacher suggested in the *American Journal of Genetics,* 2000)." Roger Robinson, ed., *Robert Louis Stevenson: His Best Pacific Writings* (Honolulu, 2003), 62.

46 First two lines from George Harrison.

47 "worlds to swing": quoted from Hugh MacDiarmid, "Empty Vessel."

"home is the sailor": RLS, "Requiem," first collected in *Underwoods* (1887), later inscribed on RLS's grave in Samoa. "home from sea" is often misquoted as "home from the sea."

48 "thinking in your inner heart": quoted from the Scottish folksong "The Road to the Isles."

Scots miles were, by traditional measurement, almost 10% longer than English miles.

50 "film director": Peter Watkins, *Culloden*, BBC, 1964.

52 "a grand memory for forgetting": the phrase Alan Breck uses to describe himself in *Kidnapped*. I used it as the title of one of my previous books of poetry (1981).

54 "over the water": Jacobite sympathizers would drink the toast to the King by holding their wine-glass above a water-glass, signifying the King "over the water," in overseas exile: i.e., Charles Edward Stuart.

"distinguished air": title of a book by Robert McAlmon (1925). Also, Henry James' "famous last words" are reported, apocryphally, to have been "So here it is at last, the distinguished thing!"

55 The statues of Sir Walter Scott and Robert Burns, both by Sir John Steel, were installed on the Mall in New York's Central Park in 1872 and 1880 respectively. So RLS certainly could have seen them on his visit to New York in 1887 (when he himself was being sculpted), though I have no proof that he did.

59 "Preparations for a Pacific voyage": as quoted in Robinson, 16.

61 "black as a footprint": all the italicized phrases in this poem, save one, come from the Gaelic folksong "Donald Ogue," as sung by Archie Fisher. The exception is "darkness is your only door," which comes from William Soutar (1898-1943).

66 RLS was a fervent supporter of Father Damien, a Belgian priest who tended to lepers at a colony on the island of Malakai, and died there in 1889. After his death, Damien's memory was attacked by a Presbyterian minister in Honolulu, who was indeed called Hyde: the Rev. Dr. Charles McEwen Hyde. RLS responded in an "Open Letter" to Hyde, a furious polemic which was widely reprinted. In it, he consistently refers to Presbyterianism as a "sect." The opening lines of this poem are borrowed from Joan Baez.

67 The marriage for one night was fictionalized by RLS in "The Beach at Falesá," in which the fraudulent document reads: "This is to certify that Uma … is illegally married to Mr John Wiltshire for one night, and Mr John Wiltshire is at liberty to send her to hell next morning." As for his own book being used in a marriage, RLS refers to it only as "a work of mine in a pirated edition" (Robinson, 87), without specifying the title — though *Jekyll and Hyde* was by far his most widely pirated book.

68 The plot of *The Master of Ballantrae* features several occasions on which the title character appears to die, only to return.

74 "Vailima": derivation of the name from Robinson, 100. Mata'afa was a Samoan chief, whom RLS vigorously supported in his struggle against a rival chief, Malieto Laupepa, who had been appointed King by the German authorities.

75 "night visitor": in many Scottish folksongs, a lover who comes at night and leaves by morning.

76 "It seemed unprovoked": the last lines that RLS ever wrote, working on the novel *Weir of Hermiston*, December 3rd, 1894. Jenni Calder:

> [RLS and Fanny] were together out on the veranda. Louis was bright with talk, the adrenalin still flowing after a good day's writing…. His hand went suddenly to his head. His fluency came to a halt with a question — "Do I look strange?" … Fanny with the help of the devoted Sosimu got him inside and on to a chair…. The extended family gathered, shocked and hushed. The doctor could do nothing but wait for the ineluctable progress of brain haemorrhage…. Shortly after eight o'clock that evening Louis died.

GLOSSARY

aa	all
Auld Reekie, Reekie	Edinburgh
awa	away
bauchle	stumble
bienly	healthy
bluid	blood
bogle	ghost
brither	brother
cairt	cart
clartie	dirty, muddy
clootie dumpling	a dumpling wrapped in cloth and boiled
close	passageway, courtyard
deid	dead
dern	dark, hidden
douce	sweet, genteel, respectable
doun	down
dour	stern, stubborn
dowie	sad, dismal
dug	dog
fash	bother
gaen	gone
gang	go
gloaming	twilight
greetin'	weeping
guid	good
haar	sea mist, fog
hodden	rough cloth
howff	public house

jinking   dodging

ken(t)   know(n)

land   tenement building
lang   long
leal   loyal
leelang   life-long
lift   sky
loon   lad

maist   most

naethin   nothing

och   oh
owrecam   chorus

plaidie   tartan cloak or shawl

snoodling   fondling, tickling: especially of animals

tenement   apartment building
thocht   thought
thole   tolerate

unco   very, exceedingly

wae   woe
wisnae   was not
wynd   narrow passage or alleyway

yir   your

ABOUT THE AUTHOR

Stephen Scobie is a Canadian poet, critic, and scholar. Born in Carnoustie, Scotland, Scobie relocated to Canada in 1965. He earned a PhD from the University of British Columbia in Vancouver after which he taught at the University of Alberta and at the University of Victoria, from which he recently retired. Scobie is a founding editor of Longspoon Press, an elected member of the Royal Society of Canada, and the recipient of the 1980 Governor General's Award for *McAlmon's Chinese Opera* (1980) and the 1986 Prix Gabrielle Roy for Canadian Criticism.